T0129523

Other Books by the Author

From the Pew to the Pulpit	Published: 08/29/2007
Isaiah 26:3-4 "Perfect Peace"	Published: 09/16/2010*
Isaiah 26:3-4 "Perfect Peace" The Last Single Digit	Published: 02/15/2012*
Isaiah 26:3-4 "Perfect Peace III" Silver and Gold	Published: 10/29/2012*
Isaiah 26:3-4 "Perfect Peace IV" The Kingdom Number	Published: 04/15/2013*
Isaiah 26:3-4 "Perfect Peace V" 2541	Published: 09/13/2013*
Isaiah 26:3-4 "Perfect Peace VI" Zacchaeus	Published: 02/28/2014
Isaiah 26:3-4 "Perfect Peace VII" Eleven	Published: 10/30/2014*
Isaiah 26:3-4 "Perfect Peace VIII" Prayer	Published: 05/21/2015*
Isaiah 26:3-4 "Perfect Peace IX" Sixteen	Published: 10/24/2015*
Isaiah 26:3-4 "Perfect Peace X" Dreams	Published: 04/12/2016
Isaiah 26:3-4 "Perfect Peace XI" Door	Published: 02/13/2017
Isaiah 26:3-4 "Perfect Peace XII" River	Published: 08/02/2017
Isaiah 26:3-4 "Perfect Peace XIII" 1 Kings 19:1-18	Published: 12/18/2017
Isaiah 26:3-4 "Perfect Peace XIV" G – Men	Published: 05/03/2018*
Isaiah 26:3-4 "Perfect Peace XV" 11:29	Published: 07/26/2018
Isaiah 26:3-4 "Perfect Peace XVI" Shoes	Published: 10/31/2018*
Isaiah 26:3-4 "Perfect Peace XVII" Arrow	Published: 01/25/2019*
Isaiah 26:3-4 "Perfect Peace XVIII" Midnight	Published: 04/26/2019
Isaiah 26:3-4 "Perfect Peace XIX" Eyes	Published: 08/20/2019
Isaiah 26:3-4 "Perfect Peace XX" Judges 4:1-16	Published: 12/18/2019

PS: On 5/25/2019, I noticed that some of the book published dates vary slightly from AuthorHouse, depending on which bookstore site you visit. They have been modified to reflect AuthorHouse's publication date, indicated by an *.

ISAIAH 26:3-4

"PERFECT PEACE XXI"

Winter

VANESSA RAYNER

authorHOUSE®

AuthorHouse™
1663 Liberty Drive
Bloomington, IN 47403
www.authorhouse.com
Phone: 1 (800) 839-8640

Published by AuthorHouse 03/20/2020

ISBN: 978-1-7283-5690-7 (sc)
ISBN: 978-1-7283-5689-1 (e)

Library of Congress Control Number: 2020905492

Print information available on the last page.

The Scriptures' quotations are taken from the KJV, NLT, ASV, DARBY, DRA, and WEB.

The King James Version present on the Bible Gateway matches the 1987 printing. The KJV is public domain in the United States.

Holy Bible, New Living Translation copyright© 1996, 2004, 2007 by Tyndale House Foundation. Used by permission of Tyndale House Publishers Inc., Carol Stream, Illinois 60188. All rights reserved. New Living, NLT, and the New Living Translation logo are registered trademarks of Tyndale House Publishers.

American Standard Version present on the Bible Gateway is in the public domain. It is a revision of the King James Version and was released in 1901.

Darby Translation present on the Bible Gateway is in the public domain. John Nelson Darby was converted in his twenties. He was an Anglo-Irish Bible teacher, one of the influential figures among the original Plymouth Brethren.

Douay-Rheims Version present on the Bible Gateway is in the public domain. It is a translation of the Bible from the Latin Vulgate into English made by members of the Catholic seminary English College, Douai, France. It is the foundation on which nearly all English Catholic versions are still based.

World English Bible present on the Bible Gateway is a public domain. It is an updated revision of the American Standard Version of the Holy Bible first published in 1901.

CONTENTS

A Gift vii
Theme ix
Prayer xi
Author's Notes...xiii
Preface.. xvii
Thanks xix
Acknowledgements xxi
Introduction xxiii
Dedication... xxv

Chapter 1   Winter 1
Chapter 2   God's Covenant with Creation...................... 4
Chapter 3   A Nation's Prayer......................... 8
Chapter 4   Lo, Winter is Past 13
Chapter 5   The LORD's Message to Cush.................. 17
Chapter 6   The LORD Speaks Doom to Israel.......... 21
Chapter 7   The 2nd Oracle.............................. 24
Chapter 8   Jesus Spoke 27
Chapter 9   The Abomination of Desolation 30
Chapter 10   The Feast of the Dedication..................... 34
Chapter 11   Paul Sails to Rome 38
Chapter 12   Paul's Travel Plans......................... 42
Chapter 13   Paul's Final Greetings 45
Chapter 14   Nicopolis 48
Chapter 15   King Jehoiakim's Winterhouse 51
Chapter 16   Wintered 55
Chapter 17   10:19 59

A Reader's Question.. 65
Author's Closing Remarks................................ 67
References 69
Answers & Information Section 73

A GIFT . . .

Presented to
_____

From
_____

Date
_____

Winter Prepares Man's Heart for Spring

THEME

The message of **Isaiah 26:3 – 4** is "Perfect Peace." This message is the distinct and unifying composition of this book with the subtitle *Winter*.

A Song of Praise

Thou wilt keep him in perfect peace, whose mind is stayed on thee: because he trusted in thee. Trust ye in the LORD for ever: for in the LORD Jehovah is everlasting strength.

Isaiah 26:3 – 4 KJV

PRAYER

Oh, Heavenly Father,
I thank you for another day and another
opportunity to write another book.
Oh, Heavenly Father, you have been good to me,
and I Thank You for all your many
blessings and your everlasting mercy.

I thank You for blessing my family.
And I pray that your people and their
families are being bless, also.
I pray that people are prospering daily in their spirit,
soul, and body by reading, Perfect Peace Books.

Oh, Heavenly Father,
I ask in Jesus' name that the Holy Spirit will
help readers to remember Your word.
I pray the word of God will give them
peace, at all times, in all situations.
Lord, I pray that your people will remember,
there is nothing too hard for you,
And you promise you will not put
more on us than we can bear.

LORD, I thank you for blessing those
that help Your work go forth.
Your word made it clear that You will
reward those that bless your servant.

It could be through prayer, words of
encouragement, to giving that person
a cup of water.

Father God,
I give you all the Glory, Honor, and Praise in Jesus' name.

Amen.

AUTHOR'S NOTES

Author notes generally provide a way to add extra information to one's book that may be awkward and inappropriate to include in the text of the book itself. It offers supplemental contextual details on the aspects of the book. It can help readers understand the book content and the background details of the book better. The times and dates of researching, reading, and gathering this information are not included; mostly when I typed on it.

2049;   Saturday, 21 December 2019; Winter begins tonight at 10:19 pm, CST.

0703;   Sunday, 22 December 2019

0426;   Tuesday, 24 December 2019

0547;   Saturday, 28 December 2019

0609;   Sunday, 29 December 2019

0807;   Tuesday, 31 December 2019; NYE Day

0618;   Wednesday, 01 January 2020; Happy New Year

2150;   Friday, 10 January 2020

0000;   Saturday, 11 January 2020

0555;   Sunday, 12 January 2020

0703;   Wednesday, 15 January 2020; I will be staying home today; Pro Shingle will be looking at my wind damaged roof that occurred early Saturday morning on 1/11/20.

0646;   Friday, 17 January 2020; I will be staying home today. Travelers Insurance Adjuster and Pro Shingle are meeting today to look at the house roof. Anyway, You Bless me, LORD; I will be satisfied! Hallelujah!

0627; Saturday, 18 January 2020

0012; Sunday, 19 January 2020

0410; Monday; 20 January 2020

0648; Tuesday, 21 January 2020

1957; Thursday, 23 January 2020

0633; Saturday, 25 January 2020

0618; Sunday, 26 January 2020

1806; Wednesday, 29 January 2020

1817; Thursday, 30 January 2020

0545; Saturday, 01 February 2020

0013; Sunday, 02 February 2020

1744; Monday, 03 February 2020

1838; Tuesday, 04 February 2020

1957; Wednesday, 05 February 2020

0705; Thursday, 06 February 2020

0515; Friday, 07 February 2020

0353; Saturday, 08 February 2020

0652; Sunday, 09 February 2020

0909; Monday, 10 February 2020

1852; Wednesday, 12 February 2020

0801; Saturday, 15 February 2020

0613; Sunday, 16 February 2020

0404; Monday, 17 February 2020; President Day

2006; Tuesday, 18 February 2020

1726; Wednesday, 19 February 2020

2007; Thursday, 20 February 2020

2101; Friday, 21 February 2020

0755; Saturday, 22 February 2020

0614; Sunday, 23 February 2020

1535; Monday, 24 February 2020

1620; Tuesday, 25 February 2020

1534; Wednesday, 26 February 2020

1909; Thursday, 27 February 2020; My Baby Sister is in town from Texas.

1333; Friday, 28 February 2020; On BCPT extended lunch break.

0749; Saturday, 29 February 2020; My cousin Verlean took my sister, Regina, and me to a restaurant called "Sweet Pea" in Bartlett, TN, yesterday evening. The home cook food was delicious!

0903; Sunday, 01 March 2020; Yesterday evening, Verlean, Regina, and I ate at Colton's Steak House & Grill. They had steak dinners. The steaks were as large as a regular-size plate. They said, the steaks were tender and juicy; basically, finger-licking good. I had a salad and baked potato with sweet tea.

2000; Monday, 02 March 2020

1736; Tuesday, 03 March 2020

1715; Wednesday, 04 March 2020

2031; Thursday, 05 March 2020

1708; Friday, 06 March 2020

0733; Saturday, 07 March 2020

1725; Tuesday, 10 March 2020

1947; Thursday, 12 March 2020

1839; Friday, 13 March 2020

0109; Saturday, 14 March 2020

0000; Sunday, 15 March 2020

1749; Monday, 16 March 2020; Looking over it again, before I sent it to AuthorHouse. Praise God.

PREFACE

Isaiah 26:3-4, "Perfect Peace XXI" Winter

The book <u>Isaiah 26:3-4, "Perfect Peace XXI" Winter</u>, is the 21st book in a series called Isaiah 26:3-4, "Perfect Peace." Hallelujah!

It all started from how I drew near to the LORD in my workplace by keeping my mind on Him. I related numbers you see throughout the day, everywhere, on almost everything on Him, His word, biblical events, and facts to give me peace in the midst of chaos.

It's our desire for you to discover the power of the Holy Spirit by numbers, words, places, people, and things surrounding the word "Winter."

Remember, the LORD Jesus <u>PROMISED us TRIBULATION</u> while we were in this world.

These things, I have spoken unto you,
that in me ye might have peace.
In the world ye shall have tribulation:
But be of good cheer; I have overcome the world.
John 16:33 KJV

However, we have been <u>PROMISED His PEACE</u> while we endure these trials, tribulations, troubles, and tests. Perfect Peace is given only to those whose mind and heart reclines upon the LORD. God's peace is increased in us according to the knowledge of His Holy Word.

> **Grace and peace be multiplied unto you**
> **through the knowledge of God,**
> **and of Jesus our LORD.**
> 2 Peter 1:2 KJV

Thanks . . . *To the Readers of the World*

As a disciple of the LORD Jesus Christ, I have learned true success comes when we are seeking and striving to do God's purpose for our lives. Our real happiness lies in doing God's will, even in the midst of our trials, tests, temptations, and tribulations, but not in fame and fortune.

Note of Interests: Trials leave us with a stronger faith in God. **Tests** allow us to see whether we can apply the word of God to live a righteous life in a sinful world. How we handle our **temptations** is a good indicator of our spiritual development. **Tribulations** are ordeals that an individual goes through, cause mostly by persecution.

I appreciate your support. Thanks for helping me spread the "Perfect Peace Series" through your e-mail, Facebook, Twitter, LinkedIn, Instagram, Tumblr, Messenger, or other accounts to your family, friends, neighbors, co-workers, church family, internet social friends, and associates.

Remember, you may not know until you get to heaven just how much a song you sung, kind words spoken by you, a book you suggested reading, or gave as a gift, at the right moment, encourage that person to keep on going when a few minutes before they were tempted to give up on life and their walk with the LORD.

Your lovingkindness to this ministry is greatly appreciated.

ACKNOWLEDGEMENTS

I wish to express my sincere gratitude to "Our Heavenly Father" for his guidance, patience, and lovingkindness throughout the writing of this book.

INTRODUCTION

For Those Who Want to Be Kept In "Perfect Peace"

This book titled, <u>Isaiah 26:3 – 4, "Perfect Peace XXI"</u> <u>*Winter*</u> was prepared and written to open your mind to a "Perfect Peace" that comes only from God. I'm striving through this book to elevate you into a "Unique and Profound" awareness of God's presence around you at all times.

According to some people, it's hard to keep your mind on the LORD. While most Christians will agree that if you keep your mind stayed on the LORD, He will keep you in "Perfect Peace." Therefore, so many people enjoy going to church on Sundays and attending midweek services for the peace and joy that they receive, but only for a short time.

You can experience the peace of the LORD throughout the day and every day. His unspeakable joy, his strength, his "Perfect Peace" during the storm, whether it's at work, home, college, school, etc. You can also experience this peace, even when your day is going well.

This concept of this book was placed in my spirit by our Father, which art in heaven, to help me when he allowed Satan to test me at my workplace until he finished molding me into a MAP; (Minister/Ambassador/Pastor).

Throughout these pages, I will be focussing on biblical events and facts surrounding "Winter." However, I am sure much more can be said concerning "Winter," so these chapter subjects serve merely as an introduction and are not exhaustive by any means.

DEDICATION

This book is dedicated to the *Winter's Lovers* . . . all over God's world.

The Sweaters Maniacs
The Boots Lovers
The Mittens with matching Hat Flaunters
The Stylist Parka Posers
The Winter Sports Fanatics:
   Skiers, Snowboarders, Hockey Players,
    Ice Skaters, Sled Riders
The Winter Festival Enthusiasts:
Dartmouth Winter Carnival in Dartmouth, New England
  Fur Rendezvous (75-mile dog sled
  racing) in Anchorage, Alaska
 International Snow Sculpture Championship
  in Breckenridge, Colorado
Madison Winter Festival in Madison, Wisconsin
Newport Winter Festival in Newport, Rhode Island
Oregon Winterfest in Cascade Mountains, Oregon
 Steamboat Spring Winter Carnival in
  Steamboat Spring, Colorado

PS: Some of the best holidays, around the world, happens during winter, right?
Three Kings Day
Winter Solstice
Christmas

Kwanzaa
New Year
Dr. Martin Luther King Day
Mardi Gras in New Orleans
Presidents Day

CHAPTER 1
WINTER

According to Genesis 1:1, "In the beginning, God created the heavens and the earth." Geoscientists have determined that the Earth God created has 3 major climate zones called Tropical, Polar, and Temperate. The 3 major climate zones can be divided into 12 smaller zones: tropical wet, tropical wet and dry, semiarid, arid desert, subtropical dry summer (Mediterranean), humid subtropical, humid oceanic (Marine West Coast), humid continental, subarctic, tundra, icecap, and highland.

The Tropical zone is the region of the earth near the equator, which include Brazil, Brunei, Cambodia, Colombia, the Republic of the Congo, the Democratic Republic of the Congo, East Timor, Ecuador, Fiji, Uganda, Kenya, Tanzania, India, Sri Lanka, Thailand, Singapore, Malaysia, Indonesia, the Philippines, Papua New Guinea, Peru, the Solomon Islands, Uganda, and Venezuela. The average temperature of the Tropical zone coldest month is 64.4 degrees in Fahrenheit.

The North and South poles have Polar climates, and in this zone, the warmest month temperature will average less than 50 degrees in Fahrenheit. The region that surrounds the North Pole is called the Arctic, which consisted of the Arctic Ocean, Asia, North America, and the northern areas of Europe.

The Temperate zone is located between the equator and the North and South poles. The Temperate Zone average temperature of the coldest month is lower than 64.4 degrees in Fahrenheit. The countries in the North Temperate Zone are Europe, Great Britain, northern Asia, North America, and northern Mexico. The countries in the South Temperate Zone are New Zealand, southern South America, South Africa, and southern Australia.

In the Tropical and Polar climate zone, the weather is ordinarily consistent throughout the year. In the Temperate climate zone, the weather is affected by warm and cold air masses at different times during the year, creating the 4 seasons known as Winter, Spring, Summer, and Autumn (Fall).

Note of Interests: Fall is the term used in Britain for the same season as Autumn, which is used mostly in American.

The coldest season of the year is Winter in the Polar and Temperate zones. The name "Winter" is an old Germanic word that means "time of water," which refers to the heavy rain and snowfall in the Winter season in middle and high latitude areas.

Winter occurs after Autumn when the axis of the Earth in the Northern or Southern Hemisphere has being oriented away from the Sun. In the Southern Hemisphere, winter occurs during the months of June, July, and August, and in the Northern Hemisphere, winter occurs during the months of December, January, and February. Winter, in many regions, is associated with snow, ice, and freezing temperatures.

Now, Winter Solstice occurs the day when one of the Earth's pole has its maximum tilt away from the sun. In the Northern Hemisphere, the winter solstice is the day with the shortest period of daylight, the longest night of the year, and the sun will be at its southernmost point in the sky. When it's winter in the Northern Hemisphere, it's summer in the Southern Hemisphere, and vice versa.

In the Northern Hemisphere, the Winter Solstice occurs typically around December 21st or 22nd, and in the Southern Hemisphere, the Winter Solstice occurs around June 20th or 21st. In 2019, the Winter Solstice occurred Saturday, December 21st, at 10:19 pm. It will happen in 2020, on Monday, December 21st. Winter is usually the months of December, January, and February, but astronomical speaking, it extends from the December Solstice to the March Equinox. The March Equinox for 2020 is Friday, March 20th.

Note of Interests: Israel is characterized as a subtropical region, between the Temperate and Tropical zone. The northern and coastal regions of Israel are hot and dry during the summer, cold and rainy in the winter, whereas an arid climate characterizes the southern and eastern areas of Israel. Only in the northernmost part of Golan Heights, near Mount Hermon is where heavy snow is found, and it remains there from December to March; in other parts of Israel, snow is rare. The city of Eilat located in the southernmost part of Israel and the northern tip of the Red Sea has a pleasant climate all year around.

CHAPTER 2

GOD'S COVENANT WITH CREATION

While the earth remaineth, seedtime and harvest, and cold and heat, and summer and winter, and day and night shall not cease.

Genesis 8:22 KJV

The word "Genesis" is a Greek word for "beginning." The Book of Genesis is the first book in the Bible, the Old Testament, and the first book of the Law of Moses known as the Pentateuch. The first sentence in the Book of Genesis begins with these words, "In the beginning."

Genesis records the beginning of time when God created the universe. The creation of heaven and earth, the creation of the fish, birds, animals, grass, trees, and humanity, are recorded in Genesis, along with the establishment of marriage, family, work, and sabbath day. Genesis records the 1st sin, murder, sacrifice, and tower. The first race, language, culture, civilization, and redemption are also mentioned in the Book of Genesis.

The Book of Genesis has 50 chapters, which can be divided into 2 parts, the primeval history in chapters 1 – 11, and the ancestral history beginning in chapters 12 – 50. The primeval history of the Bible provides a systematic understanding of the entire book of Genesis. The ancestral history of the Bible surrounds the patriarchs Abraham, Isaac, Jacob, and Joseph. The first 11 chapter of the Book of Genesis covers a minimum of 2000 years, while chapters 12 – 50 covers approximately 350 years.

Throughout the Book of Genesis, the generations of the families that populated the universe are recorded, and they are listed below.

Genesis 2:7 – Genesis 6:8	Descendants of Adam
Genesis 6:9 – Genesis 9:29	Noah
Genesis 10:1 – Genesis 11:9	Sons of Noah
Genesis 11:10 – 26	The Descendants of Shem
Genesis 11:27 – Genesis 25:11	The Descendants of Terah
Genesis 25:12 – 18	Ishmael's Descendants
Genesis 25:19 – Genesis 35:29	Isaac the Father of Esau and Jacob
Genesis 36:1 – Genesis 36:43	Esau, also known as Edom
Genesis 37:1 – Genesis 50:26	Jacob and his 12 sons

The word "winter" is mentioned first in the Book of Genesis. The Biblical event surrounding Noah is where the word "winter" is recorded in the last sentence of chapter 8, as part of God's covenant with creation, Genesis 8:20 – 22. However, the account of Noah and his family's life begins in chapter 6 of Genesis.

In brief, Noah was a righteous man in God's eyes, living on earth from 2900 BC through 1950 BC. Noah was married and the father of Shem, Ham, and Japheth. God saw how corrupt the world had become and told Noah he was going to destroy all living creatures off the face of the earth.

God told Noah to build an ark and make it 450 feet long, 75 feet wide, and 45 feet high. The ark was to have an 18-inch opening below the roof around the ark. Noah put a door on the side and build 3 decks inside the ark.

God instructed Noah to bring every kind of animal, male, and female in the ark, along with food for them. God then told Noah and his family to get into the ark because he was going to pour down rain from heaven for 40 days and 40 nights. When Noah and his family entered the ark, he was 600 years old.

Note of Interests: According to Genesis 5:32, after Noah was 500 years old, he fathered three sons named Shem, Ham, and Japheth.

———◆◆◆◆———

Noah, his wife, his sons, and their wives entered the ark on the 17th day of the 2nd month. It rained until the water covered the highest mountains on earth. God destroyed every living thing on the earth, people, livestock, small animals, beasts, and the birds of the sky. The floodwaters covered the earth for 150 days.

According to Genesis 8, God remembered Noah and all the animals with him in the ark. God sent a wind to blow across the earth, and the floodwaters begin to recede. The ark rested on the mountains of Ararat, 5 months after the flood.

Forty days later, Noah opened a window in the ark and released a raven and a dove. The raven flew back and forth until the floodwaters on the earth dried up, but the dove could find dry land because the floodwaters still covered the ground, and it returned to the ark.

Seven days later, Noah released the dove again, and it returned in the evening with a fresh olive leaf in its beak. Noah waited another 7 days before he sent the dove out again, and this time the dove didn't come back.

It was 10 ½ months after the flood began that the floodwaters had almost dried up from the earth. Noah lifted back the covering of the ark and saw that the surface of the earth was drying. God told Noah to leave the ark, release the animals so they could be fruitful and multiply on the earth.

Noah built an altar to the LORD and sacrificed burnt offerings of animals and birds. The LORD was pleased with the aroma of the sacrifice and said to himself, "I will never again curse the ground because of the human race, even though everything they think or imagine is bent toward evil from childhood. Nor will he destroy all living things. As long as the earth remains, there will be planting and harvest, cold, and heat, summer and winter, day and night, Genesis 8:21 – 22 NLT.

CHAPTER 3
A NATION'S PRAYER

You set the boundaries of the earth, and you made both summer and winter.

Psalm 74:17 NLT

The Book of Psalms is a collection of 150 psalms. A psalm is a sacred spiritual poem meant to be sung, set to a piece of music written under the guidance and inspiration of the Lord.

The Book of Psalms covers approximately 1,000 years of history. It begins with the life of Moses (1526 – 1406 BC) in the wilderness to Ezra, 4th BC. The authors of Psalms are David, Asaph, the sons of Korah, Solomon, Heman the Ezrahite, Ethan the Ezrahite, and Moses. There are about 51 Psalms in which the authors are unknown.

The Psalms of Asaph are 12 psalms: Psalm 50, and 73 – 83. Asaph was one of King David's worship leaders in the tabernacle. He was a seer, and according to 2 Chronicles 29:30, Asaph and David were excellent singers and poets.

The Book of Psalms is divided into 5 sections, which are listed below.

Section 1:   Psalms 1 – 41
Section 2:   Psalms 42 – 72
Section 3:   Psalms 73 – 89
Section 4:   Psalms 90 – 106
Section 5:   Psalms 107 – 150

The Book of Psalms is a book of prayer, praise, and perfect peace. Psalms elaborate on every imaginable thing in life. The Book of Psalms covers various ranges of human emotions, experiences, occurrences, and situations. It speaks on God's majesty, sovereignty, and creation. Psalms exalt God, encourages mankind to trust in the Lord, and to remember there is strength in him. The Book of Psalms examine the past, reflect on God's character, recall God's promises, and mankind can expect God to answer requests, and act on our behalf.

Note of Interests: There are approximately 219 Old Testament quotations used in the New Testament, and 116 of them are from the Book of Psalms. Moses wrote the 90th Psalm called "A Prayer of Moses, the man of God." This Psalm is the oldest in the Book of Psalms written around 1440 BC. Moses focused on God's greatness, our weakness, and the need for the Lord's daily provisions. Psalm 119 is an alphabetic acrostic poem and the longest psalm with 176 verses. The greatness of God's word and the affliction of man are the major themes of Psalm 119. The title given to this Psalm is "In Praise of the Law of the Lord," and this psalm reflects on suffering and difficulties in man's life. The author of Psalm 119 is not mentioned.

PS: The above information was pulled from the book title, Isaiah 26:3 – 4 "Perfect Peace XVIII" Midnight, chapter 8 by Vanessa Rayner.

The 74th Psalm was written by Asaph.

Question: Who was Asaph? *answer in this chapter . . . smile*

Psalm 74 in the KJV is numbered 73 in the Greek Septuagint Version of the Bible, and its Latin translation in the Vulgate. Psalm 74 has 23 verses, and at verse 17 is where the word **"winter"** is mention.

Psalm 74 is a passionate expression of grief, which deeply expresses the regret of the Israelites who are in Babylonian captivity. Psalm 74, also records Israelites plea for deliverance from their captives.

When King Nebuchadnezzar destroyed the temple, the psalmist asks God to think, to keep His promise, and remember the covenant. The covenant that God made with Israel was to protect them if they obeyed him.

However, the Israelites did not obey God. So, God allowed Nebuchadnezzar and his army to destroy the temple and take them into exile, Babylon. The Israelites were disheartened, devastated, and distressed because Nebuchadnezzar destroyed the temple, but they weren't sorrowful that they had disobeyed God. Therefore, God didn't have to keep his promise. Nebuchadnezzar and his army were used by God to punish Israel.

According to Psalm 74, verses 1 – 11, the psalmist records and described how King Nebuchadnezzar destroyed the temple in Jerusalem. The psalmist asked God why he is so angry with them that he allowed it to happen, and why he will not do something to rescue them.

In verses 12 – 17, the Jews praise God, remember how mighty he is, and recalls that he created and made everything on his universe.

Note of Interests: In verses 13 – 17 of Psalm 74, in the plea for deliverance, the psalmist acknowledges 7 great things God did on earth, and they are listed below.

1. Thou divide the sea by thy strength, verse 13.
2. Thou broke the heads of the dragons in the waters, verse 13.
3. Thou crushed the heads of leviathan in pieces, verse 14.
4. Thou didst cleave the foundation and the flood, verse 15.
5. Thou dried up mighty rivers, verses 15.
6. Thou hast prepared the light and sun, verse 16.
7. Thou hast set all the borders of the earth: thou hast made summer and winter, verse 17.

In the finishing verses of Psalm 74, verses 18 – 23, the psalmist ends with prayer.

Remember this,
that the enemy hath reproached, O LORD,
and that the foolish people have blasphemed thy name.
O deliver not the soul of thy turtledove unto
the multitude of the wicked: forget not the
congregation of thy poor for ever.
Have respect unto the covenant:
for the dark places of the earth are full
of the habitations of cruelty.
O let not the oppressed return ashamed:
let the poor and needy praise thy name.
Arise, O God, plead thine own cause:

remember how the foolish man reproacheth thee daily.
Forget not the voice of thine enemies:
the tumult of those that rise up against
thee increased continually.
Psalm 74:18 – 23 KJV

Note of Interests: The 74th Psalm is recited on the fast of the Tenth of Tevet in some traditions, and the 2nd day of Passover.

CHAPTER 4

LO, WINTER IS PAST

For behold, the winter is past, The rain is over, it is gone.
Song of Solomon 2:11 Darby

The 22nd book in the Old Testament is titled the Song of Solomon, KJV. Song of Solomon is also known as Song of Songs, and often referred to as merely "Songs." Song of Solomon is called after the Vulgate, the "Canticle of Canticles," and is the 47th book in the Catholic Bible, Old Testament.

Based on verse 1, chapter 1 of Song of Solomon, scholars believe King Solomon is the author, and it was written during his reign between 970 – 930 BC. Solomon's name is mentioned 7 times throughout the book; Songs 1:1, Songs 1:5, Songs 3:7; Songs 3:9, Songs 3:11, Songs 8:11, and Songs 8:12.

According to 1 Kings 4:32, Solomon wrote 1,005 songs. The title "Song of Solomon" in the Hebrew text is called "Solomon's Song of Songs." The phrase "Song of Songs" means the greatest of songs in comparison to the phrases "God of gods, Lord of lords, and King of kings; Deuteronomy 10:17, and 1 Timothy 6:15.

The Book of Song of Songs is a series of personal love poems, which gives biblical understanding concerning human love, and relationships. The poems in Song of Solomon are organized in a lengthy and beautiful dialogue between a young woman and her lover; a bridegroom who is in love with his bride. It expresses in poetic drama a maiden expression of affection between herself and her lover. The individuals mentioned in this book are King Solomon, the Shulamite maiden, and friends, KJV. In other Bible translations, the word "Shulamite" is also spelled "Shulammite."

Note of Interests: The "Shulamite maiden" is only mentioned once in the Bible, and her exact identity is unknown; Songs 6:13. However, there are Scholars with several beliefs. One of the possibilities is that she came from an unidentified place called "Shulem." Many Scholars believe Shulammite is identical to Shunammite, which is a person from Shunem, a village in the territory of Issachar. There are other Scholars who relates "Shulem" with "Salem," therefore, believing Solomon's bride came from Jerusalem. It is believed that the Shulammite woman could have been the daughter of an Egyptian king, whom Solomon married, 1 Kings 3:1. Still, others think she is the young Shunammite who served King David in his old age, named Abishag, 1 Kings 1:1 – 4.

Song of Songs is one of the Biblical Wisdom Books. It describes wisdom in a passionate and loving relationship. The love story in Song of Songs dramatically emphasizes the sanctity of marriage and reveals how marriage is blessed and consecrated in the eyes of the LORD. The Book of Songs has been viewed as an allegory of the love relationship between God and Israel, Christ and the church, and Christ and the spiritual soul of man.

Let's name the other 4 Wisdom Books of the Bible?

Smile & think . . answer in the back of the book

1. _____
2. _____
3. _____
4. _____

The Book of Song of Solomon has 8 chapters, and each chapter has less than 18 verses. The Book of Song of Solomon can be outlined as follow. In chapters 1 – 3, Solomon writes of his courtship and engagement. In chapters 3 and 4, the marriage ceremony of the bride to the bridegroom is recorded. In chapters 5 – 8, the relationship between the husband and wife, and the power of their love is spoken of.

Many waters cannot quench love, or can rivers drown it.
If a man tried to buy love with all his wealth,
his offer would be utterly scorned.
Song of Solomon 8:7 NLT

The 2nd chapter of Song of Solomon has 17 verses, and the word "winter" is mentioned at the 11th verse, speaking of a passing season of the year called "winter."

My lover said to me,
"Rise up, my darling!
Come away with me, my fair one!
Look, the winter is past, and the rains are over and gone.
Song of Solomon 2:10 – 11 NLT

Solomon loved the Shulammite, and he admired her beauty, as well as her character. The bride and groom were passionately in love. They showed respect to each other and had a harmonizing relationship between them.

Note of Interests: Scholars believe the Shulammite woman was Solomon's first and true love. According to 1 Kings 11:3, Solomon had 700 wives, princesses, and 300 concubines.

CHAPTER 5

THE LORD'S MESSAGE TO CUSH

They shall be left together unto the ravenous birds of the mountains, and to the beasts of the earth; and the ravenous birds shall summer upon them, and all the beasts of the earth shall winter upon them.

Isaiah 18:6 ASV

Cush is considered the ancestor of dark-skinned people called "Cushites." The name Cush is often associated with Ethiopia, but some Scholars are skeptical. Other scholars are still debating about the historical identity of the Cush and Cushites. However, the word "Cush" means "black." The Prophet Jeremiah calls attention to the Cushites' skin color in Jeremiah 13:23.

> **Can an Ethiopian change the color of his skin?**
> **Can a leopard take away its spots?**
> **Neither can you start doing good, for**
> **you have always done evil.**
> Jeremiah 13:23 NLT

The Cushites occupied the land of Ethiopia south of Egypt. They are described as "people tall and smooth-skinned, a people feared far and wide, an aggressive nation of strange speech, whose land is divided by rivers," Isaiah 18:2.

According to the Bible, Cush was the eldest son of Ham and grandson of Noah. The Bible doesn't name Cush's mother.

Scholars believe Cush was born around 2348 BC. Cush had 3 brothers who were named Canaan, Mizraim, and Phut. His brother Canaan was the ancestor of the tribes who originally occupied the ancient Land of Canaan, Mizraim populated the land of Egypt, and Phut inhabited the land of Ancient Libya.

Note of Interests: Scholars believe "the land of Cush" mentioned in Genesis 2:13 is most likely a different place than the "land of Cush" of later history. The later "land of Cush" is recorded as being located at the southern border of Egypt, Ezekiel 29:10.

> **The name of the second river is the Gihon;**
> **it winds through the entire land of Cush.**
> Genesis 2:13 NIV

Cush was the father of 6 sons, who were named Nimrod, Seba, Havilah, Sabtah, Sabetcah, and Raamah. The Bible doesn't mention the name of Cush's wife(s). However, the Persian historian Al-Tabari records that the wife of Cush was named Qarnabil. The mother of Cush's son named Nimrod was Semiram, the oldest daughter of Cush.

Note of Interests: Cush name is also spelled "Kush." In the Hebrew Bible, another person named Cush, a Benjamite, is mentioned in Psalm 7. He is believed to be a follower of Saul. Psalms 7:1 (Hebrew Bible) reads, "Shiggaion of David, which he sang unto the LORD, concerning Cush a Benjamite." Psalm 7 of the King James Bible doesn't have this verse, but the remainder of the verses in chapter 7 reads similarly in wordings. The only difference is that Psalm 7 of the Hebrew Bible has 18 verses, and King James Bible has 17 verses.

There are several references to Ham's son, Cush, that are only in the Old Testament. Cush was the oldest son of Ham and grandson of Noah, Genesis 10:6. Cush was the father of the "mighty warrior," Nimrod, 1 Chronicles 1:10. According to Numbers 12:1, Moses married a Cushite woman. Isaiah 11:11 states that Cush was one of the nations; the Lord recovered the remnant of his people. According to Isaiah 20:4, the King of Assyria disgraced Egypt by exposing the buttocks of the Egyptian captives and the Cushite exiles. According to Ezekiel 29:10, the land of Cush was located at the southern border of Egypt.

In the Book of Isaiah, chapter 18 is a prophecy against Cush, which occurred around 172 BC that was delivered by the Prophet Isaiah from God. The prophecy against Cush consisted of 7 verses.

In the days of the Prophet Isaiah, the region of Cush (Ethiopia) was a major world power, ruling Egypt and a chief foe to Assyria, and Judah was in the middle of the conflict between Ethiopia and Assyria. Ethiopian's ambassadors went to Judah, and the other nations of the region to make an alliance against Assyria.

According to verses 3 – 6 of Isaiah 18, God rejects the alliance with Cush, also known as Ethiopia because He is able to defend Judah against the Assyrians. If God wanted to assemble an army against Assyria, He could do it all by himself. He can annihilate the Assyrian army and leave their carcass for the mountain birds of prey.

Note, verse 6 of Isaiah 18 is where the word "winter" is embedded. According to verse 6, God said Assyria should lie upon the earth so that birds and beasts may feed upon their corpses, both summer, and winter.

> **Your mighty army will be left dead in the**
> **fields for the mountain vultures**
> **and wild animals.**
> **The vultures will tear at the corpses all summer.**
> **The wild animals will gnaw at the bones all winter.**
> Isaiah 18:6 NLT

According to the last verse of this prophecy, verse 7, Isaiah announces a day when Cush (Ethiopians) will come and worship the LORD at Mount Zion.

Mount Zion is synonymous with Jerusalem and known as the City of David. It was the highest point in ancient Jerusalem, located on the southwest side of the old city, outside the city walls. In Bible days, it was the place of Jesus' last supper and the home of the High Priest Caiaphas.

Note of Interests: Acts 8:26 – 40, speaks of Philip and an Ethiopian Eunuch, a prominent official in charge of the treasury of the "Queen of the Ethiopians." He was traveling home from Jerusalem, where he had come to worship, Acts 8:27.

CHAPTER 6
THE LORD SPEAKS DOOM TO ISRAEL

And I will smite the winter house with the summer house; and the houses of ivory shall perish, and the great houses shall have an end, saith the LORD.
Amos 3:15 KJV

The Prophet Amos was an older contemporary of the Prophets Hosea and Isaiah, during the reign of Jeroboam II in Israel, and Uzziah, also known as Azariah was the king in Judah, around 750 BC.

Note of Interests: Jeroboam II was the 13th king of the Kingdom of Israel, and he ruled 41 years. He was victorious over the Arameans, conquered Damascus, and recovered every piece of land that had been lost by Israel's ancestors, 2 Kings 14:26 – 27, 2 Kings 14:28. Economic prosperity, wealth, and luxurious living of the people occurred. This prosperity caused the collapse of moral standards and created social injustice. Idolatry spread over the country; altars were built to serve Baal and Astarte, and people even sacrificed their children on the altar to Moloch.

Amos lived among a group of shepherds from the village of Tekoa, which was approximately 10 miles south of Jerusalem. Amos makes it known in his writings; he did not come from a family of prophets, nor did he consider himself a prophet. Amos stated, he was "a grower of sycamore figs" as well as a shepherd, Amos 7:14 – 15. Amos lived in the Southern Kingdom of Judah, but he preached in the Northern Kingdom of Israel. His major prophecies were concerning social injustice, God's supremacy, and divine judgment.

The Book of Amos is the 3rd book of the 12 Minor Prophet Books in the Old Testament with 9 chapters. Amos' prophecy against Jacob's descendants is where the word "winter" is embedded in the last verse of chapter 3. In this chapter, the Lord sent Amos to deliver a message to Israel. Israel will be punished for all their sins. The enemy will surround Israel's land, break down their strong walls, and take their possessions that are hidden in the high towers.

According to the last two verses of Amos 3, which are verses 14 and 15, the Lord said, He will destroy the altars at Bethel by cutting off its horns. The winter house will be smitten along with the summer house, the houses of ivory, and the great houses.

Note of Interests: The altar at Bethel was a pagan altar, along with the altar at Dan, both built by Rehoboam, the king of Judah, according to First Kings 12:26 -30. The altars had horns at every corner, like the altar in Jerusalem. The houses of ivory were known as King Ahab's palace, 1 Kings 22:39. The winter house, as well as the summer house, were separate dwelling places for the cold and hot seasons that belonged to Kings. The winter house would be winterized, equipped with a fire burning in the brazier,

Jeremiah 36:22. The summer house was a small building, often on the grounds of the palace, built in a shady garden to provide a retreat from the summer heat. The great houses were huge mansions, enormous palaces, or gigantic living quarters.

CHAPTER 7
THE 2ND ORACLE

And it shall come to pass in that day, that living waters shall go out from Jerusalem; half of them toward the eastern sea, and half of them toward the western sea: in summer and in winter shall it be.

Zechariah 14:8 ASV

The Prophet Zechariah is the author of the Book of Zechariah. His name means "God remembered." Scholars believe that his grandfather was Iddo, who was the head of a priestly family who returned with Zerubbabel to Jerusalem. Zerubbabel led the 1st group of Jews back to Jerusalem after the Babylonian captivity, a total of 42,360 people. It is also believed that Zechariah was a priest, as well as a prophet.

Zechariah prophesied during the reign of Darius the Great after the fall of Jerusalem around 587 BC. Zechariah's contemporary was Haggai, who played an important role during the restoration of the Jewish homeland. Zechariah and Haggai both prophesied to the Jews who were in Judah and Jerusalem. Their one objective was to stir up the people to resume the work of rebuilding the Temple. Zechariah and Haggai succeeded in motivating them, and the Temple was completed 5 years later.

The Book of Zechariah is the 11th book of the 12 Minor Prophet Books. The Book of Zechariah and Hosea are the longest Minor Prophet Books, and both have 14 chapters.

The Book of Zechariah can be divided into 2 sections. Zechariah 1 – 8 is mainly concerning the rebuilding of the Temple. It was written after the Jews return from captivity in Babylon. Those chapters recall Israel's history, encourage the people to reinstate the priesthood, and obey religious laws that were forgotten during the 70-year exile. Zechariah reminded the people about the coming of the Messiah, Jesus Christ. Zechariah's 8 visions are recorded in this section, also.

The Prophet Zechariah wrote chapters 9 – 14 after the Temple was completed. Zechariah pronounced future judgment against the enemies. He declared the 1st coming of the Messiah on a donkey and mentioned the Messiah betrayal and His crucifixion. Chapters 9 – 14 also has 2 oracles. The first oracle is recorded in Zechariah 9 – 11, which outlines the course of God's providential dealings with his people down to the time of the coming of the Messiah. The 2nd oracle is recorded in Zechariah 12 – 14. The 2nd oracle points out the glories that await Israel "in the latter day."

The word "winter" is mentioned in the 2nd oracle in chapter 14. The nations that destroyed Jerusalem will be destroyed. When the destroyers of Jerusalem are destroyed, the life-giving streams will flow from Jerusalem. Half of the streams will flow to the Dead Sea in the east and the other half to the Mediterranean Sea in the west. The streams will flow continuously in both the summer and winter seasons; the streams will flow in the wet season, as well as the dry season.

There will be only one LORD who rules as King and whose name is worshiped everywhere on earth. Even the survivors from the nations that attacked Jerusalem will go to Jerusalem each year to worship the King, the LORD All-Powerful, to celebrate the Festival of Shelters, Zechariah 14:16.

Note of Interests: The Festival of Shelters (Tabernacles) is a 7-day festival, which took place on the 15th of the Hebrew month Tishri. Tishri is the 7th month on the Hebrew calendar, which usually occurs in late September to mid-October. Many scholars believe Jesus was born during the Feast of Tabernacle because it is unlikely that shepherds were still in the field with their sheep in December, which is the middle of the winter. It is most likely; the shepherds were in the fields tending sheep at the time of the Feast of Tabernacles. The Feast of Tabernacles is also known as the Feast of Booths and Sukkot, and it is the 7th and last feast that the LORD commanded Israel to observe. The Feast of Tabernacle celebrated God's continued provision for the Israelites in the current harvest. It also remembers God's provision and protection for the Israelites during the 40 years in the wilderness.

CHAPTER 8
JESUS SPOKE

And pray that your flight will not be in winter or on the Sabbath.

Matthew 24:20 NLT

The Gospel of Matthew is the 1st book of the New Testament. It was written by Matthew the Apostle, also known as Levi, Matthew the Evangelist, as well as, Saint Matthew. The primary purpose of Matthew's gospel was to prove to the Jews that Jesus is their Messiah. He records how Jesus' life and ministry fulfilled the Old Testament Scriptures. Matthew was one of the 12 disciples that were with Jesus throughout his public ministry on earth. The name "Matthew" means "gift of the LORD."

The Gospel of Matthew was written in Greek. Scholars believe it was written before 70 AD because it doesn't mention the destruction of Jerusalem, which occurred in 70 AD. The Gospel of Matthew is the 1st of the 4 gospel books, which are Matthew, Mark, Luke, and John. The Gospel of Matthew is also referred to as one of the "Synoptic Gospels" because Matthew, Mark, and Luke's Gospel include many of the same biblical stories, often in a similar sequence, and sometimes identical wordings. The 4 Gospel gives an account of Jesus' life and ministry in a specific context for a specific purpose.

The Gospel of Matthew was written for Jews. It begins with Jesus, descending directly from Abraham, a patriarch of the Jews. The Gospel of Matthew mentioned how Jesus' ministry was prophesied about in the Old Testament, and over 130 Old Testament quotes and allusions are mentioned. The Gospel of Matthew also records how Israel's Messiah, Jesus, was rejected, persecuted, and finally crucified by his people. Before Jesus was crucified, he pronounced judgment on Jerusalem, the Temple, and its leaders.

The Gospel of Matthew has 28 chapters, and in the 24th chapter, Jesus spoke and taught on the following matters.

1. Jesus Foretells the Destruction of the Temple, verses 1 – 2
2. Jesus Teaches on the Mount of Olives, verses 3 – 14
3. Jesus Spoke of the Great Tribulation, verses 15 – 22
4. Jesus Warns About False Religious Teachers, verses 23 – 28
5. Jesus Spoke of the Coming of the Son of Man, verses 29 – 31
6. Jesus' Lesson of the Fig Tree, verses 32 – 35
7. Jesus Spoke of the Unknown Day and Hour, verses 36 – 44
8. Jesus' Parable of the Faithful and Unfaithful Servants, verses 45 – 51

The 20th verse in Matthew 24, is where the word "winter" is embedded. It reads, "And pray that your flight will not be in winter or on the Sabbath." Scholars believe the reason to pray that your flight will not be in winter is that the winter days are short, unfit for long journeys, and roads are impassable. During this season, a person might encounter heavy snow, or floodwaters, making it difficult to travel, escape, or find shelter.

Note of Interests: According to the Jewish writers, the destruction of the 1st and 2nd Temple happened in the summer and not in winter. The destruction of the 2nd Temple happened on the same day Nebuchadnezzar burned down the 1st Temple, approximately 517 years earlier. The 1st Temple is also known as Solomon's Temple, and it was destroyed by Nebuchadnezzar's Babylonian Empire in 587 BC. The 2nd Temple was destroyed by the Romans in 70 AD, during the Siege of Jerusalem.

CHAPTER 9

THE ABOMINATION
OF DESOLATION

And pray ye that it be not in the winter.
Mark 13:18 ASV

The Gospel of Mark is one of the 4 gospel books in the
Bible. The other books of the gospel are Matthew, Luke,
and John. The Gospel of Mark has 16 chapters; Matthew
has 28, Luke has 24, and John has 21.

The 13th chapter of Mark is similar to Matthew's gospel,
chapter 24. The words "And pray ye that your flight be not
in the winter" are spoken by Jesus Christ recorded in the
gospels of Mark 13:18, and Matthew 24:20 KJV.

**But pray ye that your flight be not in the winter,
neither on the sabbath day.**
Matthew 24:20 KJV

The 13th chapter of Mark has 37 verses and can be outlined
as follow.

1. Jesus Foretells the Destruction of the Temple, verses 1 – 2
2. Signs and Warnings of the End of the Age, verses 3 – 13
3. The Abomination of Desolation, verses 14 – 23
4. The Coming of the Son of Man, verses 24 – 27
5. The Lesson from a Fig Tree, verses 28 – 31
6. No One Knows the Day or Hour, verses 32 – 37

In brief, after Jesus finished his teaching in the Temple courts, he left on his way with his disciples. As they were going, an unnamed disciple made remarks about the Temple and surrounding buildings, to Jesus. The unnamed disciple said, "Do you see these great buildings?"

The Temple, the unnamed disciple, is referring to is known as Herod's Temple. It was built under Herod the Great, and the construction began around 20 BC and was completed 84 years later. Scholars believe the buildings reached up to 150 ft. in height, and they were adorned with gold, silver, and precious artifacts. In Mark's gospel, the greatness of the Temple structure is emphasized, and in Luke's gospel, the Temple's beautiful stonework is highlighted.

Jesus gives his response in verse 2; he acknowledged the Temple and surrounding buildings' greatness but predicted that "not one stone will be left on another." Jesus predicts the Temple's destruction, and 40 years later, in 70 AD, the Romans ravaged Jerusalem, killed Jews, and demolished the Temple. The only stones left undisturbed were the enormous foundation stones that formed the footings for the retaining wall under the temple mount.

Note of Interests: The foundation stones can be viewed today in the "Rabbi's Tunnel," which runs north and south along the western wall. It is a portion of the western side of the retaining wall that is called the Wailing Wall.

As Jesus traveled back to the Mount of Olives, the Gospel of Mark records that Peter, James, John, and Andrew asked Jesus to tell them when these things will happen?

According to Mark 13:5 – 8, Jesus answered his disciples. He told them to take heed lest any man deceives them. There will be many that shall come saying, he is the Christ, and shall deceive many. Jesus told his disciples, they will hear of wars and rumors of wars, but don't be trouble because such things must happen, but the end shall not yet be. Then nation shall rise against nation, and kingdom against kingdom, and there shall be earthquakes, famines, and troubles, but these are just the beginning of sorrows.

According to verse 14, the disciples shall see "the abomination of desolation," spoken by the prophet Daniel. Jesus predicts a disastrous event in Judea; he said, "when you see the abomination that causes desolation standing where it does not belong, then let those who are in Judea flee to the mountains. Let no one on the housetop of his house go down nor enter the house to take anything out. The person in the field should not go back to get his cloak. It will be terrible in those days for pregnant women and nursing mothers. Pray that "the abomination of desolation" will not take place in winter, because those will be days of anguish beyond compare from the beginning, when God created the world, until now.

According to verses 17 and 18, Jesus shows his concerns for those who would be helpless when this crisis occurs. In verse 17, an unexpected journey or trying to escape would be nearly impossible for a pregnant woman. In verse 18, if "the abomination of desolation" crisis is in the winter, the food supply will be scarce, shelters will be hard to find, and riverbanks too high to cross. Jesus tells his disciples, if the LORD doesn't cut short those days, no one will survive.

After the tribulation, the sun shall be darkened, and the moon shall not give her light, and the stars of heaven shall fall, and the powers that are in heaven shall be shaken. And all shall see the Son of man coming in the clouds with great power and glory, and he shall send his angels to gather his elect from the 4 winds, from the uttermost part of the earth to the uttermost part of heaven, Mark 13:24 – 27.

Jesus ends this chapter with 2 parables, the parable of the Fig Tree, Mark 13:28 – 31, and the parable of the Servant, Mark 13:32 – 37.

CHAPTER 10

THE FEAST OF THE DEDICATION

Now the feast of the dedication was celebrating at Jerusalem, and it was winter.

John 10:22 Darby

According to John 10, the Feast of Dedication is a Jewish festival, which took place at Jerusalem, during winter. The Feast of Dedication celebrates the dedication of the 2nd temple as recorded in the books of 1st and 2nd Maccabees.

Note of Interests: First and Second Maccabees were Jewish writings concerning the history of the Jews during the events between the Old and New Testaments. These books are included in the Apocrypha and Deuterocanonical Books that are accepted by the Catholic and Orthodox Churches.

In Bible days, The Feast of Dedication was an 8-day festival, which occurred in late November or December, depending on the lunisolar Jewish calendar, starting on the 25th of Kislev. It celebrates God's protection and the victory He gave His people in the face of persecution. The Feast of Dedication began in 198 BC when the Syrian empire, King Antiochus III, took control over Judea and Samaria.

King Antiochus III son, Antiochus IV, ascended the throne in 175, and in 168 BC, he massacred many Jews, outlawed Judaism, and looted the temple. The following year, in 167,

Antiochus IV erected an altar to Zeus in the temple and sacrificed pigs on the altar. Judah Maccabee and the remaining Jews were outraged at Antiochus IV actions and led a revolt.

According to Scholars, in 165 BC, Judah Maccabee and his followers were successful in recapturing the temple. The victory over Antiochus IV began the Hasmonean Jewish kingdom.

Note of Interests: The Hasmonean Jewish kingdom lasted approximately 103 years until King Herod wiped it out around 63 BC when Jerusalem fell to Roman rule.

Once Judah Maccabee recaptured the temple, he had it cleaned, built a new altar, and had new holy vessels made. Afterward, the temple was rededicated to the LORD.

The Temple needed unadulterated, undefiled, pure olive oil with the seal of the high priest for the lampstand, which was required to burn throughout the night every night. There was only one flask of oil found, which was only enough oil to burn for one day. However, when the Jews poured in the oil and lit the lampstand, it burned for 8 days. It is this miracle that is kept alive and commemorated during the Feast of Dedication.

Today, the Feast of Dedication festival is observed by lighting the candles of a lampstand with 9 branches, called a Hanukkiah. A Hanukkiah is a special type of menorah made just for Hanukkah; it has 9 branches instead of 7 branches. The menorah is described in the Bible as the ancient Hebrew lampstand with 7-lamps and 6 branches.

Note of Interests: According to Exodus 25:31 – 32, the LORD said to Moses, "Make a lampstand of pure, hammered gold. Make the entire lampstand and its decorations of one piece – the base, center stem, lamp cups, buds, and petals. Make it with six branches going out from the center stem, three on each side. The lampstand with 7 lamps was to be kept continually burning in the holy places of the Tabernacle, Exodus 27:20 – 21.

One candle on the lampstand is lit by the special shamash candle each night until all 8 candles are lit. On the final night, the 8 days the oil lasted at the rededication of the 2nd temple is commemorated.

Psalm 30 is recited; it is an essential part of the Feast of Dedication. God gave them victory over enemies, replaced their mourning and sorrow with hope and joy is the theme of Psalm 30:1 - 12. The Hanukkah festivities include playing dreidel and eating oil-based foods, such as doughnuts and potato latkes.

PS: Psalm 30 is recorded in the back of the book for your convenience. Smile.

The Feast of Dedication has been observed and celebrated for thousands of years, rejoicing over God's protection He gave His faithful people who bravely continue to worship Him despite persecution.

The Feast of Dedication is also referred to as the Festival of Lights. According to John 8:12, Jesus declared himself, "the Light of the World." In Revelation 21, John records the New Jerusalem has no need for a sun or moon to shine, for the glory of God gives it light."

> **I saw no temple in the city,**
> **for the LORD God Almighty and**
> **the Lamb are its temple.**
> **And the city has no need of sun or moon,**
> **for the glory of God illuminates the**
> **city, and the Lamb is its light.**
> Revelation 21:22 – 23 NLT

Note of Interests: Today, this Jewish festival is known as Hanukkah and the Festival of Lights.

CHAPTER 11
PAUL SAILS TO ROME

And since Fair Havens was an exposed harbour – a poor place to spend winter – most of the crew wanted to go on to Phoenix, farther up the coast of Crete, and spend the winter there. Phoenix was a good harbour with only a southwest and northwest exposure.
Acts 27:12 NLT

The Book of Acts was written by Luke the Evangelist. The Book of Acts is viewed as a sequel to the Gospel of Luke addressed to Theophilus. Many scholars believe that Theophilus was a Greek public official and friend of Luke. Other scholars believe Theophilus is a generic term for all Christians because it means "friend of God."

The Book of Acts has 28 chapters and can be divided into 2 sections. Chapters 1 – 12 of Acts deals primarily with the history of the Church as it revolves around the ministry of Peter in Jerusalem and Samaria. Chapters 13 – 28 details Paul on his missionary journeys throughout the Roman Empire.

Beginning with the 13th chapter of Acts, Paul begins his 1st missionary journey with Barnabas. In chapter 15th, Paul and Barnabas had a disagreement concerning John Mark and parted company. Barnabas and John Mark sailed to Cyprus.

According to Acts 16, Paul's 2nd missionary journey begins with Silas, and they traveled first to Derbe. While Paul and Silas were in the city of Philippi, they were placed in prison because Paul cast a demon out of a slave girl. About midnight, while Paul and Silas were praying and singing to God, a violent earthquake shook the foundation of the prison, and the prison doors flew open. The jailer, who was keeping watch over Paul and Silas, believed in God and was saved.

In chapter 17 of Acts, while Paul and Silas were in the city of Thessalonica, Jews started a riot in the city concerning their message. Paul and Silas then travel to Corinth, and there they met Aquila and his wife, Priscilla. After Paul finished preaching, many of the Corinthians believed and were baptized.

According to Acts 19, Paul begins his 3rd missionary journey on the coast of Ephesus. Demetrius and his fellow craftsmen dragged Paul and his companions to court because they spoke against idol gods that they manufactured. In chapter 20, Paul raised Eutychus from the dead in Troas, and later the people who listen to Paul speaking accompanied him to the ship when he left for Jerusalem.

Beginning in chapter 21 of Acts, Paul journey back to Jerusalem. Paul goes to the Temple, and some Jews from the district of Asia saw Paul in the Temple, and provoked a mob against him, and grabbed him. They stated Paul was preaching against the Jewish laws, the Temple, and defiled the Temple by bringing Gentiles into the Temple. In chapter 22, Paul speaks on his experience on the road to Damascus with the LORD before the Jewish High Council.

According to chapter 23 of Acts, a group of Jews takes an oath to kill Paul. Paul's nephew tells the Roman officers, and Paul is then escorted to the city of Caesarea with armed troops to Governor Felix. Later, Paul and several other prisoners were placed in the custody of a Roman officer named Julius. They left on a ship from the port of Adramyttium on the northwest coast of the district of Asia. The ship was scheduled to make several stops at ports along the coast. When they arrived at Fair Havens Harbour, the crew member didn't want to stay there for the winter because the harbour wasn't suited for winter. They wanted to go on to Phoenix, which was farther up the coast of Crete and spend the winter there.

In an attempt, to make it to Phoenix's harbour, a storm arose; they became shipwreck and had to swim to the shore of the island Malta. In chapter 27 of Acts, next to the last chapter in the Book of Acts, is where the word "winter" is mentioned. The 27th chapter of Acts has 44 verses and can be outlined as follow.

1. Paul Sails for Rome, verses 1 – 12
2. Paul in the Storm at Sea, verses 13 – 26
3. Paul and the Crew are Shipwreck, verses 27 – 44

In the last chapter of Acts, three months after the shipwreck, Paul finally arrives in Rome. They set sail on another ship that had wintered at the Island. The ship was an Alexandrian ship with the twin gods as its figurehead.

The Book of Acts ends with Paul preaching at Rome under a guard.

So, I want you to know that this salvation from God
has also been offered to the Gentiles,
and they will accept it.
For the next two years, Paul lived in
Rome at his own expense.
He welcomed all who visited him, boldly
proclaiming the Kingdom of God
and teaching about the LORD Jesus Christ.
And no one tried to stop him.
Acts 28:28 – 31 NLT

Note of Interests: The Bible does not record how Apostle Paul died. The writings of Eusebius, an early church historian claims Paul was beheaded at the order of the Roman Emperor Nero. Paul's martyrdom occurred shortly after much of Rome burned in a fire, an event that Nero blamed on the Christians.

CHAPTER 12
PAUL'S TRAVEL PLANS

And it may be that I will abide, yea, and winter with you, that ye may bring me on my journey whithersoever I go.
1 Corinthians 16:6 KJV

Apostle Paul wrote the Book of 1st Corinthians. When Paul wrote 1st Corinthians, he was in Ephesus on his 3rd missionary journey, around 54 AD.

Corinth was known as a city of immorality, wickedness, and frivolousness. The Greek word "Corinthianize" means "to practice immorality." The primary worship of Corinth centered around Aphrodite. A temple was dedicated to Aphrodite, which housed 1,000 females who engaged in prostitution.

The city of Corinth was located on an isthmus that connected the southern part of the Greek peninsula with the mainland in the north. Corinth was the most prosperous city of mainland Greece, from 350 – 250 BC. In 146 BC, the city was destroyed by the Romans, and for 100 years, the city was left desolate. Around 44 BC, Julius Caesar rebuilt the city and settled it with Roman colonists. Corinth became the capital of Achaia in Greece.

According to Acts 18, Apostle Paul came to Corinth in 51 AD, and he stayed 18 months. During this time, the Spirit of God and its power was exhibited through Paul. Many people in Corinth were saved, and he was the founder of the church there.

After Paul left Corinth, he wrote a letter back to them, warning them not to associate with sexually immoral people, 1 Corinthians 5:9. While in Ephesus, Paul wrote a 2nd letter, which is known as 1 Corinthians, to correct problems that he heard were occurring there from the house of Chloe, 1 Corinthians 1:11.

Note of Interests: Although there are only 2 epistles to the Corinthians in the Bible, many scholars believe Paul wrote 4 letters to the Corinthian church between 51 – 56 AD, but only 2 of them survived. In both 1st and 2nd Corinthians, Paul refers to another letter; 1st Corinthians 5:9 – 11, and 2 Corinthians 2:3 – 4, 9, and 2 Corinthians 7:8, 12.

The Book of 1st Corinthians has 16 chapters, and the word "winter" is mentioned in the last chapter. The 24 verses in the 16th chapter of 1st Corinthians can be outlined as follow.

Verses 1 – 4, The Collection and Contribution for the Saints in Jerusalem
The Apostle Paul gives directions about charitable collections that need to be made in the church, for the impoverished churches in Judea.

Verses 5 – 9, Paul's Traveler Plans for Winter
Paul speaks about visiting the Corinthians. He layout his intended travel plans. He would pass through Asia, where he was staying. He would then travel through Macedonia into

Achaia, where Corinth is located. There in Corinth, Paul plans to spend time with them, and perhaps, stay through the winter.

<u>Verses 10 – 18, Paul's Request for Timothy and Stephanas</u>
Paul recommended Timothy to the Corinthians and asked them to take care of Timothy, and Stephanas, his fellow-laborers. Timothy was sent by the Apostle Paul to correct the abuses and sins which had crept in among the church of Corinth.

<u>Verses 19 – 24, Paul's Final Greetings, and Benediction</u>
Paul expresses the importance for the Corinthians to be watchful, faithful, and charitable. The Corinthians had many disputes among them, and the irregularities in teaching among them were great. There were deceivers among them, who endeavored to corrupt their faith. Paul advises the Corinthians, they should be watchful, and on their guards, always.

The Apostle Paul closed this epistle with admiration for the Corinthians. He wishes good for them, and give salutations to the church of Corinth, from the Christians in Asia, from Priscilla and Aquila, and all the brethren at Ephesus.

The grace of the LORD Jesus be with you.
My love to all of you in Christ Jesus. Amen
1 Corinthians 16:23 – 24 NIV

CHAPTER 13
PAUL'S FINAL GREETINGS

Do your best to get here before winter. Eubulus sends you greetings, and so do Pudens, Linus, Claudia, and all the brothers and sisters.

2 Timothy 4:21 NLT

Apostle Paul's final greeting is recorded in 2nd Timothy, chapter 4, verses 19 – 22. The Book of 2nd Timothy has 4 chapters, and chapter 4 has 22 verses. In Paul's final greeting to Timothy is where the word "winter" is mention. Paul is asking Timothy to visit him before winter commence. Paul wrote 2nd Timothy during his 2nd imprisonment in Rome.

Note of Interests: During Apostle Paul's 1st imprisonment in Rome, he wrote what was called the "Prison Epistles," which are named Ephesians, Philippians, Colossians, and Philemon. Paul's purpose in the Roman prison was to spread the gospel of Jesus in the Gentile capital of Rome. The Lord told Paul, "to take courage! As he had testified about Him in Jerusalem, he must also testify about Him in Rome," Acts 23:11.

Second Timothy is one of the 3 Pastoral Epistles written by Paul; the other two are First Timothy and Titus. These 3 epistles are called Pastoral Epistles because they relate to the conduct of church leaders, focus on organization, and leadership within the household of God. The Pastoral Epistles are delivered to and addressed to Timothy and Titus. Timothy was over the church in Ephesus, and Titus was over the church on the Island of Crete.

When Paul wrote the second letter to Timothy, the young pastor had been ministering to the church at Ephesus for 4 years. The city of Ephesus was a major port city in Asia Minor in the 1st century. Timothy was a faithful servant to Paul ever since he had left home with the Apostle Paul, more than a decade earlier.

Timothy's father was Greek, and his mother was Jewish. Timothy's mother, Eunice, and grandmother, Lois, were both Christian believers. The Apostle Paul met Timothy during his 2nd missionary journey in Lystra around 50 AD. He was unmarried and about 33 years old, and Paul was 48 years old. Paul decided to take the young Timothy with him as he travels preaching the gospel because of recommendations made by several church members, Acts 16:2. Timothy's name means "honoured by God," and Paul addressed Timothy as "my true son in the faith," 1st Timothy 1:2.

Note of Interests: Once Timothy was ordained by Paul and church brethren, he ministered in at least 5 New Testament churches, 1 Thessalonians 3:1 – 2, 1 Corinthians 4:17, Philippians 2:19 – 22, Acts 17:14, and 1 Timothy 1:3. Catholic traditions record that Timothy died in Ephesus when he was around 80 years old. Scholars believe Timothy, the Bishop of Ephesus, was murdered when he told a crowd of pagans that their idolatrous celebrations were foolish.

Timothy had ministered alongside Paul for the duration of both Paul's 2nd and 3rd missionary journeys in Troas, Philippi, Corinth, and Ephesus. Timothy was trusted by others to carried money collected by the Philippian church to care for Paul's needs in Corinth. Paul testified to those in Philippi regarding Timothy Christian character, and his dedication to spreading the gospel, Philippians 2:20 – 22.

Paul wrote to Timothy, a young pastor in the church at Ephesus, to provide him with encouragement in the face of difficulties and trials. When Paul was in prison, he summoned his faithful friend Timothy to come to see him before winter, for a farewell visit, 2nd Timothy 4:21.

Paul wrote 2nd Timothy, just before his death in 67 AD by the Roman emperor Nero. Scholars believe that 2nd Timothy is the last epistle Paul wrote before his death, addressed to Timothy, a faithful friend, and a fellow missionary.

CHAPTER 14

NICOPOLIS

I am planning to send either Artemas or Tychicus to you. As soon as one of them arrives, do your best to meet me at Nicopolis, for I have decided to stay there for the winter.
Titus 3:12 NLT

❖✦❖

The Book of Titus is one of the Pastoral Epistles written by Apostle Paul; the other two are 1 Timothy and 2 Timothy. Titus has only 3 chapters, and Paul wrote this letter to Titus, a Greek-speaking Gentile believer, to instruct and encourage him. Titus was in leadership over the church on the Island of Crete, which is the largest island in Greece.

Titus accompanied Paul on his 3rd missionary journey. Scholars believe that Titus was converted by Paul either in Antioch or Syria around 43 AD. Others believe that Paul converted Titus on his first missionary journey in Pamphylia or Galatia around 47 AD.

In 49 AD, Paul took Titus with him to attended the Council of Jerusalem. There Paul asked the leaders in Jerusalem to take the decision not to require non-Jewish believers to be circumcised, and the leaders agreed with Paul, Acts 15. Paul's letter to Titus was written shortly after Paul's first letter to Timothy, which contains some of the same instructions and advice.

Titus helped Paul at Ephesus during his 3rd missionary journey. Titus was sent from Ephesus to Corinth with Paul's first letter to the Corinthians. Afterward, Titus took good news about the Corinthian church back to Paul at Philippi, 2 Corinthians 7:6 – 7. Titus then took Paul's second letter to the Corinthians from Philippi to Corinth, 2 Corinthians 8:16 – 17.

In 62 AD, after Paul was released from house arrest in Rome, Titus traveled with Paul to Crete, and there Paul left him in charge of the new church. The Church of Agios Titos in Irakieio, Greece, commemorates the appointment of Titus to oversee the Cretan church.

Later, Paul asked Titus to meet him in Nicopolis. The word "Nicopolis" only occurs once in the Bible, Titus 3:12. The city, Nicopolis, was the capital of the Roman province of Epirus Vetus located in the western part of Greece. The city was founded by Caesar Augustus in 29 BC.

On September 2, 31 BC, Augustus was victorious over Antony and Cleopatra at the Battle of Actium. Nicopolis was known as the "city of victory. Caesar Augustus made Nicopolis an important trade center on the region of Epirus. He resettles citizens of nearby cities to this location. In 27 BC, Caesar transferred his Roman Stadium to Nicopolis, where the Actian Games were held to commemorate his victory.

Nicopolis quickly became the metropolis of Epirus, with the freedom to govern itself, according to Greek customs. But in the time of Emperor Julian around 362 AD, the city had fallen into decay. It was plundered by the Goths, who were early Germanic people, and later restored by Justinian the Great around 527 AD, and finally disappeared entirely in the Middle Ages.

According to Titus 3, Paul wrote a letter to Titus delivered by Artemas or Tychicus between 63 – 65 AD. He urges his young friend in the ministry to meet him in Nicopolis, where he was going to spend winter.

Scholars believe Paul may have intended to start a church on the western coast of Greece. Scholars also believe Nicopolis is the city where Paul was arrested and taken to Rome for trial during one of the winters, between 64 – 67 AD.

CHAPTER 15
KING JEHOIAKIM'S WINTERHOUSE

Now the king was sitting in the winter house in the ninth month; and there was a fire in the brazier burning before him.

Jeremiah 36:22 WEB

King Jehoiakim was the king, who was sitting in the winter house in the 9th month. He was the 18th king of Judah from 609 to 598 BC. Jehoiakim was the 2nd son of King Josiah and Zebidah. Jehoiakim's father, Josiah, was a king that pleased God, Jeremiah 26:1. King Josiah returned Judah to the Lord, tore down idol altars, and restored obedience to God's law, 2 Kings 23.

Note of Interests: In the Hebrew Bible, Kislev is referred to as the 9th month of the Jewish calendar, and 3rd month of the Gregorian calendar. The month of Kislev signal the arrival of the winter season in the Holy Land. Kislev is the month in which the 1st rainbow was observed after the Flood.

Once King Josiah died, his son named Jehoahaz was chosen king by the people. Jehoahaz did not follow in the righteous footsteps of his father, Josiah. Jehoahaz did evil in the sight of the LORD. He reigned for 3 months before he was taken into captivity by King Nebuchadnezzar of Egypt. Jehoahaz was then replaced with his brother Eliakim, 2 Kings 23.

The king changed Eliakim's name to Jehoiakim, who was 25-year old.

King Jehoiakim did evil in the sight of the LORD. God sent armies to capture and enslave them because of Judah's ongoing sins. King Jehoiakim was taken captive by King Nebuchadnezzar and taken to Babylon, 2 Kings 24.

Note of Interests: Daniel and his 3 friends were also taken to Babylon during this time, Daniel 1:1 – 2. Daniel's friends were Hananiah, Mishael, and Azariah, whose names were changed to Shadrach, Meshach, and Abednego.

King Jehoiakim was later returned to Jerusalem by King Nebuchadnezzar but had to pay Nebuchadnezzar tributes. During the time King Jehoiakim reigned as a vassal of Babylon, the prophet Jeremiah prophesied in Jerusalem. The message was that the Babylonian invasion was God's punishment for Judah's sins, and they should repent.

King Jehoiakim decided he wanted Jeremiah's scroll read to him in his court. He sent his officer, Jehudi to Elishama, the secretary's room where the scroll was kept. Jehudi returned with the scroll and begun to read it to the king. King Jehoiakim was in his winterhouse, which is described as a winterized part of the palace. He was sitting in front of a fire to keep warm.

Note of Interests: The KJV Bible at Jeremiah 36:22 uses the word "winterhouse," to describe where King Jehoiakim was sitting when the scroll was read. Other Bible translation uses the following word or words in place of "winterhouse."

Winter-house, ASV
Winter-house, DARBY
Winter house, DRA
Winterized part of the palace, NLT
Winter house, WEB

As King Jehoiakim was listening to the words from the scroll, each time Jehudi finished reading 3 or 4 columns of the scroll, he would cut them off with the scribe's knife and throw them into the firepit. King Jehoiakim continue this process until the entire scroll was burned in the fire. The king and his servants, who heard these words showed no fear, nor did they tear their clothes, Jeremiah 36.

However, Elnathan, Delaiah, and Gemariah begged the king not to burn the scroll, but he wouldn't listen. The king then commanded his son Jerahmeel, Seraiah son of Azriel, and Shelemiah son of Abdeel to arrest Baruch and Jeremiah, but the LORD hid them.

Note of Interests: King Jehoiakim murdered the prophet, Uriah, because he prophesied against his wrongdoings, Jeremiah 26:20 – 23.

Jeremiah rewrote the scroll that King Jehoiakim burned, and God pronounced judgment on him. The LORD says that Jehoiakim king of Judah will have no one to sit on the throne of David, and his body will be exposed to the heat by day and the frost by night. Jehoiakim will be buried like a dead donkey, dragged out of Jerusalem, and dumped outside the gates. When Jehoiakim stopped paying tribute to Babylon, this prophecy was fulfilled. King Jehoiakim reigned for 11 years.

After Jehoiakim's death, his son Jehoiachin succeeded him as the new king of Judah. He was 8 years old when he began to reign, and he reigned only 3 months and 10 days before he was taken to Babylon, 2 Chronicles 36.

King Nebuchadnezzar then made Zedekiah his brother king over Judah and Jerusalem. Zedekiah did what was evil in the sight of God, and he refused to listen to the words of God given by the Prophet Jeremiah. When Zedekiah rebelled against King Nebuchadnezzar, he killed the men of Judah, carry away the treasures in the Temple, burned the Temple, and tore down the walls of Jerusalem. The message spoken by Jeremiah was fulfilled.

According to scholars, in October 539 BC, Cyrus of Persia captured mighty Babylon. In the 1st year of King Cyrus of Persia, the LORD stirred the heart of Cyrus to put this proclamation in writing, and he sent it throughout his kingdom. This is what King Cyrus of Persia said:

> **"The LORD, the God of heaven, has given
> me all the kingdoms of the earth.
> He has appointed me to build him a Temple
> at Jerusalem, which is in Judah.
> Any of you who are his people may go there for this task.
> And may the LORD your God be with you!"**
> 2 Chronicles 36:23 NLT

CHAPTER 16

WINTERED

And after three months we departed in a ship of Alexandria, which had wintered in the isle, whose sign was Castor and Pollux.

Acts 28:11 KJV

The word "wintered" is a simple past tense and past participle of the verb "winter." The word "wintered" means to spend the winter in a particular place or location. Scholars believe the word "winter" derives from the Proto-Germanic word "wentruz," which means "winter." Proto-Germanic is the root of all Germanic languages and was spoken during the time of the Roman Republic, and the Roman Empire, until the 1st century.

The word "wintered" mentioned in Acts 28:11 is associated with Paul's life and ministry. The Book of Acts is the 5th book in the New Testament, and it is also referred to as "The Acts of the Apostles," and the 5th gospel by others. The Book of Acts continues to record the events surrounding the spread of Christianity in the 1st century, beginning with Jesus' ascension to Heaven.

The Book of Acts has 28 chapters, which can be divided into 2 sections. The first section deals primarily with the ministry of Peter in Jerusalem and Samaria in chapters 1 – 12 of Acts. The second section records Paul on his missionary journeys throughout the Roman Empire, Acts 13 – 28.

Beginning in Acts 13, Barnabas and Paul start their first missionary journey. Paul pronounces judgment on Elymas, the sorcerer, and he goes blind. Many people believed in Paul and Barnabas' teaching and were added to the church.

According to chapter 14 of Acts, signs, and wonders are done by Paul and Barnabas. Paul heals a lame man in Lystra, who was crippled from birth. Later, Paul is stoned and left for dead. The disciples of Paul gathered around him and prayed, and Paul is then restored to life.

According to Acts 15, Paul and Barnabas set out for their 2nd missionary journey. In chapter 16, Paul meets Timothy and takes him along on his missionary trip. Paul encourages the church, and the church increases in believers. The Holy Spirit forbids Paul to preach in Asia and Bithynia. Paul receives a vision to go to Macedonia in northern Greece. Paul cast out an evil spirit of divination from a slave girl, which earned her master a lot of money. Afterward, Paul and Silas were dragged and placed in jail. Around midnight Paul and Silas were praising and worshiping God, and an earthquake shook the foundation, and the prison doors were open. The jailer and his household believed in the LORD Jesus and were saved.

According to Acts 17, Paul and Silas traveled through the towns of Amphipolis, Apollonia, and then Thessalonica. The Thessalonians study and search the scriptures, and many believed in the LORD Jesus Christ and were saved.

According to Acts 18, Paul became acquainted with a Jew named Aquila and his wife Priscilla, and they became believers. In chapter 19, Paul sets out on his 3rd missionary journey. Paul ministered in Ephesus. God gave Paul power to perform miracles. Demetrius and the craftsmen started a riot against Paul.

According to Acts 20, Paul raised Eutychus from the dead after falling from a window. According to Acts 21, after Paul arrives at Jerusalem, he is arrested in the Temple.

According to Acts 22, Paul tells of his conversion on the road to Damascus. In chapter 23, the LORD appears to Paul at night and told him to be encouraged, and he must preach the Good News in Rome. In chapter 24, Paul appears before Felix, and he is touched by Paul's speech, but he let Paul remain in prison.

According to Acts 25, Paul witnesses to King Agrippa. In chapter 26, Paul speaks of his conversion to Festus and Agrippa. They agreed that Paul hadn't done anything to deserve death or imprisonment, and he would have been set free if he hadn't appealed to Caesar.

According to Acts 27, Paul sails for Rome with other prisoners. Paul warns shipmates of the dangerous trip. An angel of God appears to Paul, telling him that he would grant safety to everyone sailing with him.

Acts 28 is the last chapter in the Book of Acts. This chapter is where the word "wintered" is mentioned in verse 11. Acts 28 mentioned Paul survives a fatal viper bite on the Island of Malta, verses 1 – 7. In verses 8 – 9, Paul heals Publius' father, who was sick with fever and dysentery. Then all the other sick people on the island came and were healed by Paul.

According to verse 10, the people of the island showered Paul and the ship crew with gifts, supplies, and everything they needed for their trip when it was time to sail. Paul and the shipwrecked crew had stayed at the island for 3 months until an Alexandrian ship was ready to set sail after staying at the island during the wintertime.

In verses 24, Paul preached anointed sermon and more believed the gospel.

According to Acts 28, verses 17 – 30, for 2 years, Paul preached and lived in Rome under guard. He welcomed all who visited him, bolding proclaiming the Kingdom of God and teaching about the LORD Jesus Christ, and no one tried to stop him.

CHAPTER 17

10:19

According to Channel 5, Meteorologist R. Childers, Winter officially began for the year 2019, on Saturday the 21st of December, at 10:19 pm, CST. This chapter will list all the books in the Bible that have chapter 10 and verse 19. I pray that each verse encourages you to take time, in your study time, to read the whole chapter.

Old Testament

The Old Testament is the 1st section of the KJV Bible. It has 39 books which cover the history of the world and focus on creation, Abraham, the Patriarchs, Moses, the Exodus, Joshua, the Conquest of Canaan, the Judges, David, Solomon, the divided kingdom, the destruction of Israel/Judah, Ezra, and Israel return from captivity.

Genesis
And the border of the Canaanites was from Sidon, as thou comest to Gerar, unto Gaza; as thou goest, unto Sodom, and Gomorrah, and Admah, and Zeboim, even unto Lasha.

Exodus
And the LORD turned a mighty strong west wind, which took away the locusts, and cast them into the Red sea; there remained not one locust in all the coasts of Egypt.

Leviticus

And Aaron said unto Moses, Behold, this day have they offered their sin offering and their burnt offering before the LORD; and such things have befallen me: and if I had eaten the sin offering to day, should it have been accepted in the sight of the LORD?

Numbers

And over the host of the tribe of the children of Simeon was Shelumiel the son of Zurishaddai.

Deuteronomy

Love ye therefore the stranger: for ye were strangers in the land of Egypt.

Joshua

And stay ye not, but pursue after your enemies, and smite the hindmost of them; suffer them not to enter into their cities: for the LORD your God hath delivered them into your hand.

1 Samuel

And ye have this day rejected your God, who himself saved you out of all your adversities and your tribulations; and ye have said unto him, Nay, but set a king over us. Now therefore present yourselves before the LORD by your tribes, and by your thousands.

2 Samuel

And when all the kings that were servants to Hadarezer saw that they were smitten before Israel, they made peace with Israel, and served them. So the Syrian feared to help the children of Ammon any more.

1 Kings
The throne had 6 steps, and the top of the throne was round behind: and there were stays on either side on the place of the seat, and 2 lions stood beside the stays.

2 Kings
Now therefore call unto me all the prophets of Baal, all his servants, and all his priests; let none be wanting: for I have a great sacrifice to do to Baal; whosoever shall be wanting, he shall not live. But Jehu did it in subtilty, to the intent that he might destroy the worshippers of Baal.

2 Chronicles
And Israel rebelled against the house of David unto this day.

Ezra
And they gave their hands that they would put away their wives; and being guilty, they offered a ram of the flock for their trespass.

Nehemiah
Hariph, Anathoth, Nebai,

Job
I should have been as though I had not been; I should have been carried from the womb to the grave.

Proverbs
In the multitude of words there wanteth not sin: but he that refraineth his lips is wise.

Ecclesiastes

A feast is made for laughter, and wine maketh merry: but money answereth all things.

Isaiah

And the rest of the trees of his forest shall be few, that a child may write them.

Jeremiah

Woe is me for my hurt! my wound is grievous; but I said, Truly this is a grief, and I must bear it.

Ezekiel

And the cherubims lifted up their wings, and mounted up from the earth in my sight: when they went out, the wheels also were beside them, and every one stood at the door of the east gate of the LORD's house; and the glory of the God of Israel was over them above.

Daniel

And said, O man greatly beloved, fear not: peace be unto thee, be strong, yea, be strong. And when he had spoken unto me, I was strengthened, and said, Let my lord speak; for thou hast strengthened me.

The books of Ruth, Song of Solomon, Lamentations, Joel, Amos, Obadiah, Jonah, Micah, Nahum, Habakkuk, Zephaniah, and Haggai in the Old Testament doesn't have a 10th chapter. The books in the Old Testament that have a 10th chapter, but no 19th verse are Judges, 1 Chronicles, Esther, Psalm, Hosea, and Zechariah.

<u>New Testament</u>

The New Testament is the 2nd section of the KJV Bible; Christian biblical canon. Many scholars believe that most of the New Testament books were written between 50 – 95 AD. The New Testament has 27 books, which are accredited to 8 different authors. Six of the 8 authors are numbered among the Apostles, which are Matthew, John, Paul, James Peter, and Jude, and the other two are their immediate disciples named Mark and Luke. The New Testament records the birth, life, teachings, ministry, death, and resurrection of Jesus Christ. It also records the events of 1st century Christianity.

<u>Matthew</u>
But when they deliver you up, take no thought how or what ye shall speak: for it shall be given you in that same hour what ye shall speak.

<u>Mark</u>
Thou knowest the commandments, Do not commit adultery, Do not kill, Do not steal, Do not bear false witness, Defraud not, Honour thy father and mother.

<u>Luke</u>
Behold, I give unto you power to tread on serpents and scorpions, and over all the power of the enemy: and nothing shall by any means hurt you.

<u>John</u>
There was a division therefore again among the Jews for these sayings.

Acts
While Peter thought on the vision, the Spirit said unto him, Behold, three men seek thee.

Romans
But I say, Did not Israel know? First Moses saith, I will provoke you to jealousy by them that are no people, and by a foolish nation I will anger you.

1 Corinthians
What say I then? That he idol is any thing, or that which is offered in sacrifice to idols is any thing?

Hebrews
Having therefore, brethren, boldness to enter into the holiest by the blood of Jesus.

The books in the New Testament that doesn't have a 10th chapter are Galatians, Ephesians, Philippians, Colossians, 1 Thessalonians, 2 Thessalonians, 1 Timothy, 2 Timothy, Titus, Philemon, James, 1 Peter, 2 Peter, 1 John, 2 John, 3 John, and

Jude. The books of 2nd Corinthians and Revelation are the only two books in the New Testament that have a 10th chapter, but no 19th verse.

A READER'S QUESTION

This new section just dropped in my spirit at 0613 on January 14, 2017, titled <u>A Reader's Question.</u>

Question: How do I choose the next title for the next book?

Answer: I believe almost every book title is explained how it came about in the Author's Note Section. If I remember correctly, some book title subjects were dreamt or seen over and over throughout the weeks. There have been subject matters dropped in my inner being, constantly stayed on my mind, and lightly spoken to me by Father God, I believe. Hallelujah!

**In all thy ways acknowledge him,
and he shall direct thy paths.**
Proverbs 3:6 KJV

AUTHOR'S CLOSING REMARKS

Praise God! I must be honest in Jesus' Name, "At first, I had the hardest time writing this book! I just couldn't get motivated. I missed writing for days and even a week, and when I did write on this book, I would only work on it about an hour or less, not the usually 3+ hours. I questioned God about writing this book numerous times. I asked God, where this the right subject matter, or did I misunderstand Him, or is it time to do something else for 2020?"

Praise God! When I made up my mind to stop questioning God and "Fast," Father God reveal to me what the issue was, even though I fell twice before I succeeded with the "3-day Fast." Hallelujah!

Subconsciously, I had my mind and heart inclined to write another book, similar to the one I had just written, titled: Isaiah 26:3 – 4 "Perfect Peace XX" Judges 4:1 – 16. I asked Father God to forgive me. When I repented, the desire and energy were restored to me, Hallelujah, God is an understanding and wonderful God!

As I meditated on the word "Winter" and sincerely read and studied the events surrounding the word "Winter," my understanding was enlightened, and my soul was blessed. I pray Isaiah 26:3 – 4, "Perfect Peace XXI" Winter is a blessing to your mind and heart, soul and spirit, bone and marrow.

Pray for the Ministry . . .

May the "Prince of Peace," Bless you and give you "His Peace."

Dr. Vanessa

REFERENCES

Chapter 1
1. BibleGateway: https://www.biblegateway.com
2. Wikipedia, The Free Encyclopedia: https://en.wikipedia.org/wiki/Winter

Chapter 2
1. BibleGateway: https://www.biblegateway.com
2. Jacksonville Theology Seminary: Genesis

Chapter 3
1. BibleGateway: https://www.biblegateway.com
2. Wikipedia, The Free Encyclopedia: https://en.wikipedia.org/wiki/Psalm_74

Chapter 4
1. BibleGateway: https://www.biblegateway.com
2. Jacksonville Theology Seminary: Song of Songs

Chapter 5
1. BibleGateway: https://www.biblegateway.com
2. Wikipedia, The Free Encyclopedia: https://en.wikipedia.org/wiki/Cush

Chapter 6
1. BibleGateway: https://www.biblegateway.com
2. Wikipedia, The Free Encyclopedia: https://en.wikipedia.org/wiki/Amos
3. Jacksonville Theology Seminary: The Minor Prophets

Chapter 7
1. BibleGateway: https://www.biblegateway.com
2. Jacksonville Theology Seminary: The Minor Prophets

Chapter 8
1. BibleGateway: https://www.biblegateway.com
2. Jacksonville Theology Seminary: The Synoptic Gospels

Chapter 9
1. BibleGateway: https://www.biblegateway.com
2. Jacksonville Theology Seminary: The Synoptic Gospels
3. Wikipedia, The Free Encyclopedia: https://en.wikipedia.org/wiki/Mark_13

Chapter 10
1. BibleGateway: https://www.biblegateway.com
2. Jacksonville Theology Seminary: Biblical Festivals
3. Wikipedia, The Free Encyclopedia: https://en.wikipedia.org/wiki/Menorah_(Temple)

Chapter 11
1. BibleGateway: https://www.biblegateway.com
2. Wikipedia, The Free Encyclopedia: https://en.wikipedia.org/wiki/Paul_the_Apostle
3. Jacksonville Theology Seminary: Peter and Paul

Chapter 12
1. BibleGateway: https://www.biblegateway.com

Chapter 13
1. BibleGateway: https://www.biblegateway.com
2. Wikipedia, The Free Encyclopedia: https://en.wikipedia.org/wiki/Second_Epistle_to_Timothy

Chapter 14
1. BibleGateway: https://www.biblegateway.com
2. Wikipedia, The Free Encyclopedia: <u>https://en.wikipedia.</u><u>org/wiki/Nicopolis</u>

Chapter 15
1. BibleGateway: https://www.biblegateway.com
2. Wikipedia, The Free Encyclopedia: <u>https://en.wikipedia.</u><u>org/wiki/Jehoiakim</u>
3. Jacksonville Theology Seminary: Biblical Kings

Chapter 16
1. BibleGateway: https://www.biblegateway.com
2. Wikipedia, The Free Encyclopedia: <u>https://en.wikipedia.</u><u>org/wiki/Acts_of_the_Apostles</u>

Chapter 17
1. BibleGateway: https://www.biblegateway.com

ANSWERS & INFORMATION SECTION

Chapter 4
1. Psalms
2. Job
3. Proverbs
4. Ecclesiastes

Chapter 10
Psalm 30 has 12 verses.
A psalm of David. A song for the dedication of the Temple.
1. I will exalt you, LORD, for you rescued me. You refused to let my enemies triumph over me.
2. O LORD my God, I cried to you for help, and you restored my health.
3. You brought me up from the grave, O LORD. You kept me from falling into the pit of death.
4. Sing to the LORD, all you godly ones! Praise his holy name.
5. For his anger lasts only a moment, but his favour lasts a lifetime! Weeping may last through the night, but joy comes with the morning.
6. When I was prosperous, I said, "Nothing can stop me now!"
7. Your favour, O LORD, made me as secure as a mountain. Then you turned away from me, and I was shattered.
8. I cried out to you, O LORD. I begged the LORD for mercy, saying,
9. "What will you gain if I die, if I sink into the grave? Can my dust praise you? Can it tell of your faithfulness?

10. Hear me, LORD, and have mercy on me. Help me, O LORD."
11. You have turned my mourning into joyful dancing. You have taken away my clothes of mourning and clothed me with joy,
12. that I might sing praises to you and not be silent. O LORD my God, I will give you thanks forever! NLT

Printed in the United States
By Bookmasters